Original title:
Chasing Life's Meaning with a Cup of Tea

Copyright © 2025 Creative Arts Management OÜ
All rights reserved.

Author: Colin Harrington
ISBN HARDBACK: 978-1-80566-073-6
ISBN PAPERBACK: 978-1-80566-368-3

Serendipity in a Saucer

A cup of joy spills on my desk,
Sugar's a boggart, the spoon's a risk.
Laughter dances on tea leaves brown,
While socks wander off, never to be found.

The kettle whistles a curious song,
I sip the warmth, and it feels so wrong.
In a world where everyone's in a race,
I find my fortune in this messy place.

Tea-Stained Chronicles

Once I brewed a cup of green,
It turned out brown and fit for a queen.
A teabag's saga, a water's fling,
In the chaos, I find my zing.

Earl Grey whispers in a playful tone,
Like a cheeky cat who's left alone.
I muse through sips, some dreams are heard,
And pen my thoughts in a weekly word.

Sipping Through Seasons

Winter's chill with a peppermint kiss,
I sip, I slip, oh what is this?
Spring brings blossoms and a party hat,
Where tea and giggles sit down to chat.

Summer's ice with a zesty twist,
Cooler than troubles that coquette and twist.
Autumn's leaves spiral down for tea,
A pumpkin spice giggle just for me.

Memories Wrapped in Steam

In the steam a ghost dances by,
A memory stirred with a curious sigh.
Was it you who spilled all that cream?
Or that cat who thought it could redeem?

Whispers of laughter float in the air,
As I sip and question, do I even care?
The mug's a portal to odd tales told,
With every sip, my heart's uncontrolled.

Fragments of Comfort

A kettle whistles, oh what joy,
It wakes the hopes of every boy.
With clumsy hands, I spill some leaves,
Tea stains my dreams, but who believes?

Sip and sigh, the world's a mess,
Yet in my cup, I find my dress.
A splash of milk, a sprinkle sweet,
Turns my kitchen into a treat.

The Steeping Story

Leaves dance and swirl in water warm,
A tempest brews, a perfect storm.
I try to wait, but oh, it's tough,
Patience, my friend, can feel so rough!

Each drop whispers tales long past,
Of tea with friends, and jokes that last.
Laughter rises, tea cups clink,
In this moment, we hardly think.

Foamy Fantasies

Oh glorious foam, a crown so tall,
Riding my cup, I'm having a ball.
A sip reveals a world untold,
Where biscuits dance and dreams unfold.

This brew's a friend, it likes to tease,
With every gulp, I'm weak in knees.
Unicorns join, and gnomes all cheer,
In my fevered mug, they're always near!

The Essence of Each Pour

Pour it slow, let magic flow,
In every cup, new tales to sow.
With silly faces, we take a seat,
Discussing life while munching a treat.

Do the leaves roll their eyes, I wonder?
As we sip stories, there's joy to ponder.
The clock ticks loud, but here we stay,
Finding meaning in crumbs of clay!

Warmth in a Porcelain Embrace

In a cup so round, I find my dreams,
Searching for answers, or so it seems.
My thoughts steep slow, in this cozy brew,
Is it the tea, or is it just you?

Sipping my fears with a spoonful of honey,
Feeling quite wise, or maybe just funny.
Each sip a riddle, wrapped in a joke,
Maybe the pot's gone and lost to the smoke.

Leaves of Wisdom

Dancing around like leaves on the floor,
Brewing up thoughts that I can't ignore.
With every pour, my worries dissolve,
What life's about? Well, who knows? Let's evolve!

Tea with a twist of lemon and cheer,
Sharing my secrets with the kettle, I hear.
If wisdom's at the bottom of this cup,
I'll just keep sipping, never give up!

Infusions of Introspection

Stirring the pot, I ponder the day,
Is this a journey? Or a silly ballet?
With giggles and bubbles, the steam clouds my mind,
In this playful dance, all my thoughts unwind.

I blend my regrets with ginger and spice,
Each flavor a lesson, some sweet, some not nice.
Catch the giggles, hold on to the calm,
The meaning of life? It's a warm, tasty balm!

A Quiet Moment in Time

In quiet moments, I sip and I think,
Of the joys of hot drinks, and the riddle they ink.
The clock ticks softly, as my heart finds its beat,
Wrapped in warm thoughts, life feels bittersweet.

Tea leaves swirl like memories in my cup,
Each color a note, in a symphony up.
So here's to the laughs and the quiet delight,
Finding my meaning, one sip at a night!

The Philosophy of a Brew

In the morning light, I sip with glee,
Thoughts bubble up like a stormy sea.
Each drop holds wisdom, each sip a clue,
A mug of deep thoughts, a comedy brew.

The kettle sings tunes of existential dread,
Should I be wise, or just stay in bed?
Earl Grey or chamomile, a vibrant debate,
Over bitter leaves, I ponder my fate.

Moments of Mindfulness

I meditate on my mug's warm embrace,
Is happiness brewed or brewed with grace?
Lost in the swirl of my fragrant blend,
I laugh with the leaves, my giggling friend.

Pouring tea like I'm filling my soul,
Stirring my troubles down deep in the bowl.
Biscuit in hand, life's complexities flee,
As I sip on simplicity, carefree like me.

The Language of Leaves

The leaves chatter softly, like old-time pals,
Sharing their secrets in herbal salves.
Matcha whispers wisdom, chai spins a tale,
In this brewed comedy, I silently sail.

Green tea's a skeptic, black tea's quite bold,
Oolong just giggles, with stories retold.
With each playful sip, I ponder the stars,
Are the bubbles of foam simply cosmic avatars?

Serenity Stirred

With a twist of the spoon, my worries comply,
As steam curls upward, my thoughts take to fly.
A dance of serenity in each gentle swirl,
My teapot's philosophy, like life, in a whirl.

Caffeine nudges wit, as sugar delights,
I chuckle in sips, as life takes flights.
Tea stains my mug, but lessens my strife,
In this brew of jokes, I find joy in life.

Journeys in a Teacup

I brewed a cup, a steamy delight,
In my cozy kitchen, morning light.
With little leaves swirling, oh what a scene,
Do they whisper secrets or care what I mean?

I sip the warmth, it tickles my nose,
In my porcelain boat, where adventure flows.
Each sip is a giggle, each gulp a new quest,
What wisdom can froth bring? Who needs a rest?

My cup's a magician, with tricks up its sleeve,
Transforming my worries, making me believe.
"Life's short," it tells me, "just lighten the mood,
With a sip of this magic, don't brood, don't brood!"

In the saucer's embrace, I dip my sweet treat,
What joy can be found in chocolate, so neat?
As teabags dance wildly and lemons take flight,
I laugh at the chaos—what a silly sight!

So join me, dear friends, let's steep tales anew,
In a world full of flavors, and laughter is due.
With a teacup as vessel, let's sail through the day,
For life's just a brew, in a quirky display!

Mugs and Musings

In my cozy nook, I sip and think,
Pondering life over a brew that's pink.
The kettle hums, a quirky song,
Wondering where I went so wrong.

With every slurp, wisdom is sought,
A side of giggles, a dash of thought.
The leaves unfurl, stories they weave,
In my cup, the answers deceive.

Oh the chaos of pour and sip,
As I try to decipher this wild trip.
Do I seek fortune or just more tea?
Is the meaning just missed, or simply glee?

Each mug a mystery, a riddle to solve,
In the world of blends, I must evolve.
Life's a steep, with flavors so bright,
Let's brew up joy, it'll be alright!

Journeying through Flavors

With every brew, I travel afar,
To lands unknown, without a car.
Green hills, brown roots and chamomile dreams,
Exploring the world in steam and creams.

A citrus twist makes me giggle loud,
While oolong whispers from the crowd.
Herbal paths lead me to delight,
As I sip my way through day and night.

Lost in blends, I dance with spice,
Jasmine winks, oh isn't she nice?
Each cup holds secrets, adventure untold,
In the dance of flavors, I feel bold.

So I pour another, a daring leap,
Into the cup, where wishes creep.
A sip of laughter, a dash of cheer,
In this brew, my worries disappear!

Threads of Serenity

In the stillness, I find my thread,
A fragrant brew beside my bed.
With each sip, the laughter flows,
As I ponder where the weirdness goes.

Earl Grey grins with a cheeky smile,
While chai winks, inviting me for a while.
Tangled in flavor, I snicker and muse,
Finding serenity in steamy clues.

Each swirl a wonder, each sip a laugh,
Tea leaves back stories like an old photograph.
With warmth in my hands, I'm lost in the fold,
As life's little quirks are lovingly told.

In this cozy bubble, I'll linger long,
With a sip here and there, I can't go wrong.
Threads of joy knit into my heart,
With each cup shared, we're never apart!

Liquid Contemplation

With a teacup full of quirky thoughts,
I dive into flavors, connecting the dots.
Each drop a giggle, a silly game,
In the world of brew, nothing feels lame.

Black tea chuckles, green tea sings,
As I ponder all life's strange little things.
Infusions of laughter, a pinch of glee,
Pouring my heart into this cup, you see.

The world spins faster while I just sip,
Finding deep meaning in every drip.
Lemon zests up my ponderous stare,
In this liquid dance, I feel so rare.

So let's brew joy in a vibrant swirl,
With a twist of whimsy, let's give it a whirl.
Life's a steeped adventure, come join the spree,
Where every sip is a new decree!

Unfolding Stories

In the morning light, I brew my cheer,
The kettle sings, it's music to hear.
With each sip I ponder, like a wise old sage,
Is this just tea or life's next page?

Cream or sugar, oh what a choice,
Though my belly rumbles, I still rejoice.
The teabag flaps like a tiny flag,
Declaring war on my inner nag.

Tales from the Teacup

Once a leaf, so green and bright,
Now dances in hot water, pure delight.
Each swirl unleashes a story or two,
Of how I spilled tea on my new shoe.

A splash of milk makes me feel so grand,
Like a queen with a cup in hand.
The biscuits tremble, they're next in line,
To be dunked and then vanished, oh how divine!

The Brewed Journey

With every sip, I travel afar,
To lands with no traffic, just sun and a star.
My teacup brims with laughter and glee,
Who knew the journey was this carefree?

I've met many mugs, both bold and shy,
Some with slogans that caught my eye.
But they never spill secrets, what a shame,
Just sit by and watch as I play this game.

Peace in the Infuser

I seek tranquility in a ceramic shrine,
Brewing adventures in water and time.
The infuser whispers, 'What's your next quest?'
I answer, 'Find cookies and take a rest!'

A sip of this, and I'm ready to go,
To live each moment, let the good times flow.
For in this cup, I find my escape,
Dancing with flavors, a hilarious fate.

Brewing the Unseen

In a kettle boiling bright,
We search for answers day and night.
With each steep, the world does swirl,
Trying to find our own lost pearl.

Lemon zest and ginger's kick,
Stirring thoughts that come so quick.
Is it wisdom? Or just the spice,
In this cup, what's the price?

A sip reveals the secrets bold,
A story in each drop untold.
Do we find joy in hazy steam?
Or just another half-baked dream?

With friends around, the laughter flows,
As we ponder life's highs and lows.
One more cup, let's dive right in,
Is it fortune, or just caffeine?

Steeping in the Unknown

In the shadows where the teabags hide,
We ponder life, not just the ride.
Should we steep or should we strain?
Maybe add some chocolate rain?

Mugs are clinking, jokes are made,
Between the laughs, fears start to fade.
With each slurp, we ponder so,
Are we brewing deep thoughts, or just a show?

What's the meaning—no clue in sight,
Is that a teacup or a dialogue fight?
Herbal or black, should we dare
To dive into the humble fare?

As the kettle sings its song,
We sip and suspect we belong.
Swap out questions, swap out glee,
What was that? Tea, or irony?

Whispers in a Teapot

In a teapot worn but spry,
Whispers swirl like dreams on high.
What's brewing under steam and heat?
Just life's musings, oh so sweet.

A little honey makes it clear,
While sitting with friends who cheer.
What's the question? Pass the cream,
Is it folly or is it a dream?

Cupped hands hold a world of chatter,
Each sip reveals what really matters.
Is the meaning in the leaves or mug?
Or perhaps in a friendly hug?

So as we sip and find our jam,
In the cozy that's a sham,
Let's laugh and ponder while we drink,
Is this hot brew just a wink?

Steeping Dreams

The kettle's gurgling, dreams arise,
With each pour, the future flies.
One sip closer to understanding,
Or maybe just misbanding.

Caffeine dances in our heads,
Ideas bloom like flowerbeds.
Did I just brew the cosmic tale,
Or the leftovers in the pail?

Rolling laughter, quiet thought,
In this blend, insight is sought.
With each bubble that comes to greet,
Is this brew or a mental feat?

So fill your cup, embrace the quest,
Together we rise—you know the rest.
With dreams in hand, we cheerfully sip,
In this teacup, let's take a trip.

Aroma of Understanding

In a cup, a riddle brews,
Beneath the steam, I read the clues.
Each sip, a puzzle, a twist of fate,
Tasting wisdom, I contemplate.

Laughter bubbles, oh what a sight,
With marshmallows dancing in the light.
Sweet peppermint whispers, 'Take your time,'
I spill deep thoughts, like lemon-lime.

With a tea bag's charm, I find my groove,
In this porcelain world, I make my move.
Sipping on giggles, sipping on dreams,
Life's meaning is sweeter than it seems.

As my mug warms up my chilly hands,
I sip with glee, my heart expands.
Aroma of joy fills the air,
With each giggle, I shed my care.

Time in a Teacup

Clocks tick softly, time feels slow,
In my jade teacup, wisdom flows.
With each swig of this perfect blend,
I ponder if time has a funny end.

A swirling dance of leaves and dreams,
Reality unravels at the seams.
Earl Grey giggles, Chamomile sighs,
In this merry brew, nothing defies.

Biscotti crumbles, a crunchy cheer,
Pour me more, I'm starting to steer!
Through the milky way, on a tea-stained trail,
Bringing back laughter with such detail.

The kettle whistles a playful tune,
Whirling thoughts beneath the moon.
In this delicate dance, we twirl and sip,
Finding meaning with a chuckle and a quip.

Rituals of Resonance

Tea leaf disciples gather round,
To sip the truth that's steeped profound.
We swirl our cups like fortune tellers,
In laughter, we're the great mind dwellers.

A teapot's whisper, a kettle's shout,
In this cozy den, we sip and pout.
Pumpkin spice giggles, chai-hugging tight,
Unraveling mysteries with each light bite.

Friendship brews in a porcelain bowl,
Echoing laughter tugs at my soul.
With lemon zest and a side of fun,
We realize this journey's just begun.

We toast to the chaos, we raise a glass,
With every sip, the moments pass.
In memories laced with sugar and cream,
We unravel existence, sip on the dream.

Sips of Serenity

A sip of calm, oh what a glee,
Drowning my worries with herbal tea.
Chamomile giggles as tension flees,
A cozy corner where thoughts can tease.

Dancing flavors, a pot filled wide,
In every cup, a little joy we bide.
With every sip, I loosen the strings,
The harmony of laughter blissfully clings.

Sugar and spice, a twist of fate,
In the land of tea, I am never late.
To cozy corners where stories bloom,
Embracing life amid the sweet perfume.

So here's to sips with friends so dear,
With every pour, the world feels near.
In a teacup's universe, we find our cheer,
Painting our moments, perfectly clear.

Fables of Flavorful Brews

In the kettle, stories swirl,
Where leaves dance and flavors twirl.
Each sip, a giggle, a chuckle or two,
Brewing laughter, just me and you.

The secrets of life in a mug so fine,
With each hot drop, we laugh and dine.
The world slows down, the steam does rise,
Over tea, we uncover the wise.

Tea bags sigh, while sugar sings,
Life's little joys are the simplest things.
A splash here, a pour there,
Who knew there'd be such flair?

So let's toast to cups that brim with cheer,
And giggles shared with friends so dear.
In every sip, a fable brewed,
In every moment, life's subtly rude.

Tasting the Unwritten

A teacup holds potential vast,
In every steep, a spell is cast.
With cookies on the side, oh dear,
Life tastes better with a little cheer.

What plots unfold with each warm sip,
Like secret notes, on a friendship trip.
We sip and plot our silly schemes,
Tea leaves whisper, a duo of dreams.

Who knew chamomile knew the drill?
Or Earl Grey's wisdom could be such a thrill?
Each brew a tale, both wild and sweet,
We craft our stories, one cup, repeat.

So let's drink deep, the unwritten tales,
Where humor brews and laughter prevails.
With tea in hand, our hearts take flight,
Together we sip through the night.

Cups of Quietude

In the calm, with a mug in tow,
We ponder life, then spill the flow.
Spices dance, and we snicker and sip,
Finding humor in every little quip.

A quiet moment, a sneaky grin,
As cream swirls, where chaos spins.
In the haven of tea, we softly sigh,
Discussing why the teapot is shy.

Notes of jasmine and tales of yore,
Each fill brings laughter, who could ask for more?
We contemplate why socks disappear,
And laugh as we sip, oh dear, oh dear!

So let's brew a storm of gentle wit,
In every cup, let's do our bit.
For in the silence, the fun is found,
With cups of quietude, we laugh profound.

An Invitation to Reflect

Gather around, the cups are hot,
Join in the fun, with laughter a lot.
Pour that tea, let's indulge in cheer,
Who knows what wisdom will appear?

In every sip, a riddle unfurls,
As tea leaves swirl like dancing pearls.
We clink our mugs, a joyous sound,
And in that moment, peace is found.

Tiny pastries make marvelous hosts,
Telling a tale in buttery toasts.
Each giggle shared brews camaraderie,
As we sip life's mystique, oh so free.

So raise your cup, don't hesitate,
For in this brew lies our fate.
An invitation to let joy reflect,
As we drink deep, savor and connect.

The Pour of Possibility

In the kettle's dance, we place our bets,
A splash of hope, and forget regrets.
Brew laughter strong, let the giggles steep,
A cup of dreams is ours to keep.

Stir the chaos with a gentle hand,
Mix the flavors, oh, isn't life grand?
Take a sip, let the stories unwind,
Each drop invites the curious mind.

When the world gets grim, add more cream,
And watch the swirl become a dream.
With every pour, the moments tease,
In this warm brew, we find our ease.

So here's a toast with a clumsy clink,
To life and tea, the perfect link.
Raise your cup, let the giggles flow,
In the steam and laughter, we both grow.

Sip of the Soul

In the morning sun, the cup takes flight,
A potion strong to ward off fright.
With every sip, a chuckle grows,
The secret's out, it's in the flow.

Pour the joy, let worries drip,
In the teacup, take a dip.
Puns on the side, with ginger zest,
A soul revived, we're truly blessed.

The leaves are swirling, so are we,
A whimsical whirl, oh, can you see?
With every gulp, a giggle blooms,
In mugs of life, let fun consume.

So let's confess, it's more than tea,
It's laughter shared, just you and me.
So cheers to sips and playful souls,
In tiny cups, we reach our goals.

Moments in a Matcha

Whisk the green with a playful flair,
Add a dash of joy, no need to care.
In the frothy swirl, a smile appears,
Each glug a laugh, melt down your fears.

With every sip, we taste the fun,
The matcha's glow, our hearts are spun.
Sprinkle some humor on top of foam,
In this crazy brew, we find a home.

Let's spill the tea on silly plights,
Giggles arise in the morning light.
Matcha's a muse with every taste,
In this playful art, there's never waste.

So grab your cup and raise it high,
With each sip, let the laughter fly.
In moments shared, let's dance and play,
With matcha dreams lighting the way.

Harmony in Handcrafted Brews

Crafted with care, each blend's a joke,
A dash of curiosity, a wink, a poke.
Pouring warmth into cups, oh what a sight,
This merry potion makes everything bright.

From chamomile calm to chai's spicy cheer,
Each flavor a story we hold dear.
Stirring the pot with laughter's embrace,
Living our lives in a joyful race.

When the teapot whistles, we gather near,
To share our tales, our joy, our cheer.
A handcrafted brew, a toast to the night,
In these joyful cups, everything's right.

So here's to the brews that make us grin,
With tea in hand, let the fun begin.
Raise your mugs high, let the laughter ring,
In every sip, life's a vibrant spring.

In Search of the Perfect Brew

I wandered through the tea shop's maze,
Hoping to find a drink that pays.
One bag said 'energy', the other 'relax',
My brain spun round, thanks to the snacks.

The barista laughed at my confused stare,
Said, 'Just pick a flavor, if you dare!'
I brewed a leaf that danced with glee,
But ended up with a cup of misery.

The strainer whistled like a kettle's song,
I took a sip, but it felt so wrong!
'This blend's a mystery, a comedy show,
Best leave it be, let's stick to coffee, though.'

With herbal notes and fragments of joy,
My search continued like a curious boy.
Next time I'll ask for the wildest brew,
Or just buy a bottle, that's easier too!

The Dialogue of Leaves and Water

The leaves would scoff, with tales to share,
'Water, you're dull, without a flair!'
'But I get heated, make you come alive,'
Said the water, in a bubbling dive.

'You're just a dried-out, crunchy mess!'
The leaves replied with odd finesse.
'You need my spices for some class,
Or else you'll stay as just a glass!'

Together they brewed in a pot so round,
Creating warmth from the chaos found.
'You're sweet and nice, but quite the tease,'
Stir in some milk and I'll feel at ease!

Thus their banter turned rather smooth,
With smiles and scents, they danced and moved.
In their teacups, a friendship bloomed,
As laughter escaped from the flavor-filled room!

Each Sip, a New Horizon

First sip sparks joy, a quest anew,
Earl Grey dreams or a fruity stew?
The cup sways gently, giggles arise,
As I ponder life 'neath the cloudy skies.

The chamomile whispers sweet, 'take it slow',
While peppermint shouts, 'Let's steal the show!'
Every taste is a journey, a funny ride,
My senses awaken, I cannot hide.

Oh, the oolong clouds, float softly by,
With each little drop, I'm destined to fly.
Caffeine makes me dance, a jig so spry,
With laughter and joy, I could touch the sky!

Yet the herbal notes sometimes make me yawn,
'Too soothing,' I say, as daylight's drawn.
But in this cup, adventure unfurls,
Each sip a new story, with giggles and twirls!

Solace in a Semblance

In a fragile cup, my thoughts convene,
They brew together, creating a scene.
'This life is like tea', the mug would confess,
'A splash of chaos, yet still, we bless!'

Each steep reveals a glimpse of fate,
The dregs of worries that I overstate.
A splash of lemon or perhaps some spice,
Mixing up troubles, oh isn't life nice?

With scented dreams and a warm embrace,
Tea comforts me in this madcap race.
I sip, I laugh, I feel so free,
A merry moment, just tea and me!

Though the kettle may whistle and sometimes cry,
I find my solace with leaves on high.
In every bubble, a joke resides,
Life feels lighter, with tea as my guide!

Tea Time Reveries

In a cup, I seek the tales,
Of lost socks and windy trails.
The tea leaves dance, a silly sight,
Spilling secrets day and night.

I ask the mug, what's life's big joke?
It chuckles back, then starts to smoke.
Do biscuits hold the key, I wonder?
Or is it just a sweet day's blunder?

With every sip, I feel so wise,
As steam ascends, my spirit flies.
A swirl of cream, a dash of fun,
Is the answer hidden? I've just begun!

So here I sit, with leaves and dreams,
In my teapot, life's quirks gleam.
Pour another round, let giggles flow,
In every drop, a chance to grow.

Pouring Over the Present

Pouring tea, I ponder fate,
When did I start to procrastinate?
Each sip is like a playful tease,
Am I wise, or just at ease?

The kettle whistles with such grace,
Yet here I am, a slow-paced race.
With every cup, the world expands,
I try to grasp with clumsy hands.

I spill some tea, a splash of truth,
My inner child claims eternal youth.
The drips and drops, my only guide,
A syrupy path where giggles reside.

Life's lemonade in a fine china cup,
"Don't worry, friend, just drink it up!"
Each visit's a riddle, a joy, a jest,
Pour another cup, let's see the rest!

Whispers in a Teacup

In the bottom of my cup, I spy,
A world that laughs as time goes by.
The sugar's grinning, the milk's aglow,
What wisdom emerges, I hardly know.

A quickened heartbeat with each warm sip,
I wrangle thoughts that bubble and slip.
"Is tea the elixir?" I query aloud,
The cup replies with a perky cloud.

An infuser's whimsy spins tales anew,
Of dragons, muffins, and a caffeinated zoo.
My teapot gurgles, can't keep it still,
Life's a chuckle, a whimsical thrill.

With a flourish, I sip, then I slurp,
Finding answers in each tiny burp.
Cheers to the moments, both sweet and absurd,
In the whispers of tea, life's quirks are heard!

Steam Rising

Steam's rising high, like dreams in flight,
With every pour, the morning's bright.
My cup is filled with giggles fair,
Each sip reveals a secret layer.

Hot tea whispers in a playful tune,
While sugar sputters like a cartoon.
I keep my spoon like a fancy wand,
Stirring laughter into my fond.

The kettle hums a cozy song,
While life's absurdities dance along.
In the brew, I glance, I muse a bit,
Laughing at things that don't quite fit.

So pour those leaves and brew that cheer,
In every cup, the fun is near.
Sharing warmth with friends and tea,
Life's a carnival, come and see!

Thoughts Falling

Thoughts fall like leaves, gently steeped,
In the whirl of the world, I've leaped.
A sip of whimsy, a dash of mirth,
In every bubbling drop, I flirt.

My teacup's rim holds stories grand,
Of unspoken truths and a busy hand.
With laughter bursts, the leaves take flight,
Each delightful drop, a ticklish bite.

As the world stirs, I find my pace,
With every gulp, a warm embrace.
Is that wisdom or just caffeine?
In this kaleidoscope, what's truly seen?

So let us feast on sips of cheer,
With every cup, we draw near.
When life's absurd, let's raise a mug,
Wit and warmth in every hug!

Mysteries of Leaf and Water

I steep my thoughts in boiling brew,
As leaves swirl round in a leafy hue.
What wisdom lies in this fragrant mug?
A hint of citrus or cozy snug?

The kettle whistles secrets loud,
Of ancient sages and a teacup crowd.
I sip and ponder, make silly faces,
For life's big questions can hide in places!

Each sip is like a riddled jest,
With tea as my guide, I feel more blessed.
Shall I add honey or lemon zest?
Ah! The answer lies where I'll happily rest!

So here I sit, with cup in hand,
Curious leaves for the thoughts I planned.
A sip of laughter, a dash of care,
With tea, my troubles float in the air!

Heartbeats in Earl Grey

In a cozy café with scones on plate,
I ponder the world, while I oscillate.
What winks from the steam of this lovely tea?
Could it be the secrets of blissful glee?

The Earl Grey beckons with bergamot flair,
I swirl in daydreams of feathers and air.
Do teabags whisper or brew in jest?
Or is it me, just sipping my quest?

With biscuits crumbling in damp delight,
Life's trivial matters can feel quite light.
A slurp and a giggle, I sip, I twirl,
While inside my mug, all my thoughts unfurl.

Heartbeats in cups, laughter's old friend,
Where introspection and fun blend.
So raise your teacup, embrace the cheer,
Here's to life's giggles, brewed crystal clear!

The Brewed Odyssey

Once upon a kettle, in the great unknown,
I set forth on journeys from my lovely throne.
With leaves as my compass, and water my map,
Adventures await in this aromatic lap!

The hibiscus sings, while oolong plays coy,
Each sip a story, like a curious toy.
What do they know of the sun and the moon?
Swirling in flavors, oh, how I swoon!

Green tea giggles with an earthy glee,
While chai's warm embrace feels like a hug to me.
I traverse these realms with a playful grin,
For simplicity shines where the good vibes begin.

So here's to the brews, the journeys we take,
In porcelain hearts, love's flavors awake.
Every sip, a tale, every cup, a spark,
In this brewed odyssey, adventures embark!

Tea and the Tides of Thought

The waves of my mind ebb and flow with the brew,
As I dip my teabag, in oceanic hue.
Rolling tides of flavors, a salty surprise,
What wisdom is found in these cerulean skies?

The chamomile whispers soft lullabies,
With each droplet's dance, my laughter complies.
Do thoughts swim with fishes, or maybe with whales?
Navigating sea storms with lemony sails?

In my cup, a tempest or serene little lake,
With ripples of humor for goodness' sake!
I ponder the currents, the sails on the breeze,
With every hot sip, my worries freeze.

So let's sail together, tea's treasures in tow,
With whimsical dreams, just watch us glow!
In the tides of reflection, we swig and we sway,
For nurturing laughter is the best sort of play!

Unraveling Threads of Time

In a tiny cup, I sit and muse,
Stirring thoughts like sugar cubes.
What day is it? I've lost the hour,
Time slips by, like sugar power.

With a splash of milk, my mind takes flight,
Floating dreams, oh, what a sight!
Lost in thought, the kettle sings,
Oh, what joy a teacup brings!

Each sip, a giggle, each gulp, a grin,
Spill some tea, let the chaos begin.
What's this flavor? A mix of fun,
A brew that dances in the sun.

As the leaves unfurl, so do my plans,
Mapping adventures with tiny hands.
Who needs depth when you've got cheer?
Let's toast this cup and chug some fear!

The Harmony of Honey and Hopes

Pour in the honey, sweet and gold,
Like sticky laughter, bold and old.
My worries float on a syrupy sea,
As I sip dreams of who I could be.

What's that? A dab of ginger too?
A kick of spice, to stir my view.
Let the steam rise and waft in glee,
As visions swirl, just like my tea.

So raise your cup to the silly plight,
Of overthinking every bite.
In this dance of brews and laughs,
We sip our hopes, let joy be our paths.

With laughter echoing through the air,
Life's a brew, if you just dare.
So let's concoct a cup divine,
And toast to tales, both yours and mine!

Gathering Clouds in a Teacup

A storm brews in my porcelain friend,
Clouds of thoughts that twist and bend.
What's the weather? I ponder long,
With each sip, I feel so strong.

Teabags steeping, a scented tease,
Hold on tight, it's sure to please.
I stir my fears with a gentle swirl,
What chaos brews in this mad world?

Look at that! A lemon slice!
A zesty twist—the best advice.
Let's squeeze the day, full of zest,
And see which clouds we can digest.

As the last drop lingers, I sigh with glee,
Each sip a journey, wild and free.
What if the answer was honeyed bliss?
Let's brew another, nothing amiss!

Captured Moments, One Sip at a Time

The clock ticks slowly, like molasses,
Each moment savored as the teapot passes.
A slurp, a giggle, oh, what a scene,
Every drop counts, if you know what I mean!

Where's the rush? In this cozy nook,
Spinning tales over the recipe book.
Let the kettle whistle our great escape,
Life's all about that cup-shaped shape.

With each sip taken, wisdom grows,
What happens next? Who really knows?
Between sips of laughter and crumbs of pie,
We stumble on answers, oh me, oh my!

So here's a toast with each little brew,
To moments saved and friendships true.
In this quirky dance of tea and cheer,
Let's sip life gently, year after year!

Brews of Reflection

In a cup of leaves, my thoughts steep,
I ponder my dreams, though they're not that deep.
With every sip, my worries dissolve,
Like sugar cubes in a mystery to solve.

The kettle whistles a cheerful tune,
I dance in the kitchen, a joyous buffoon.
Life's puzzles seem simpler, oh what a feat,
As I sip on this brew, isn't life sweet?

My friends come knocking, mugs in their hands,
We sip and we laugh, making quirky plans.
Between sips of tea, we pretend to be wise,
But mainly we giggle, oh, how time flies!

In the end, the quest feels delightfully clear,
It's the laughter we share, and of course, the beer—
Oh wait, I meant tea, it's a wonderful craze,
Life's meaning resides in these frothy displays.

The Essence of Warmth

With a teabag's embrace, I sit with glee,
What's the meaning, I wonder, oh tea, set me free!
Each drop in the cup whispers tales from the leaf,
I chuckle at life and its cheerful mischief.

A biscuit dives in, oh what a splash,
The meaning of munching? Just make it a trash!
Warmth spreads through my core, like a hug from a cat,
Who knew the answers came with a chat?

In my comfy chair, the mysteries whirl,
I'm a philosopher now, with crumbs all a-twirl.
Silly thoughts dance as I sip, oh so slow,
Does wisdom come sipping, or just watching the show?

Life's questions simplify, in this cozy retreat,
With each little gulp, I find joy can't be beat.
Put on your kettle, let's solve it with cheer,
The essence of warmth is simply being here!

Leaves Unraveled

Loose leaves on the table, a curious sight,
They tell me their secrets, but not every night.
With a swirl in my cup, they laugh and they tease,
Finding out life's puzzles is a breeze, if you please!

Each swirl tells a story, sometimes it's a joke,
I snicker at life, just some whimsy and smoke.
What do I see in this steaming delight?
Wisdom's just waiting, but first, take a bite!

Tea parties happen, where logic gets tossed,
Every sip is a gamble; what's gained is not lost.
As my friends spill their woes, in giggles we drown,
Those leaves have the answers; let's drink and not frown!

And when the last drop meets the bottom so clear,
I toast to the leaves, and I cheer with my beer!
Though truth may elude, in laughter we drown,
The leaves keep unraveling, with joy, we renown.

Serenade of Sips

A chorus of cups serenades every heart,
In the rhythm of sipping, we all play a part.
With laughter as music, we fill up the air,
Life's crazy questions drift with nary a care.

Each slurp and each gulp brings a story to tell,
As tea leaves infuse, our giggles compel.
Every drop seems to echo, 'Why so serious, friend?'
When the best of life's lessons come steeped to the end!

The kettle hums softly, a sweet lullaby,
As I ponder my purpose while making a pie.
With marshmallow fluff and a dash of good cheer,
It's perfect for pondering—oh, my dear!

So lift up your cups, let's toast with delight,
To questions unasked and vague dreams in sight.
In the serenade's echoes, we find the grand cause,
It's sipping together, applause after applause!

Dancing with Dialogue

In the corner cafe, a voice did croon,
With every sip, thoughts danced 'round the room.
The cups chattered secrets, oh what a tune!
Got wisdom from tea leaves, but none from the broom.

Laughter bubbled up, like steam from the pot,
Talking to biscuits, in a grand little spot.
They giggled and laughed, oh what a knot,
In a tea party world, where logic's forgot.

Cups of Curiosity

Pouring a cup, my thoughts took flight,
What if the teabag could talk all night?
I asked it questions, with great delight,
It whispered back softly, 'You're doing alright!'

The sugar cubes giggled, 'We're sweet and we're bold!'
They shared the stories that never get old.
I asked them to dance, and they did it uncontrolled,
Living like legends, their adventures retold.

The Quietness in a Kettle

The kettle sings softly, a bubbling hum,
Waiting for whispers, and a few jokes to come.
While water swirls in, I ponder and strum,
Does the kettle know secrets? Or is it just numb?

A teacup chimes in, 'I soak up the cheer!'
It beams with excitement, 'It's good to be here!'
With a splash and a giggle, I've nothing to fear,
For laughter and warmth are what I hold dear.

Threads of Time in Tea

With each cup I sip, the clock seems to freeze,
Time unravels gently, 'Oh, do as you please.'
Moments intertwine like the leaves in the breeze,
While I sip my good fortune amidst all my teas.

The teapot spills tales of the days long gone,
Of dragons and slippers, of dusk until dawn.
And I chuckle to myself, as I sip and yawn,
For in this tea world, I am never withdrawn.

Wisdom in Each Sip

Pour it hot, let it steep,
A brew of dreams, not too deep.
With each gulp, thoughts arise,
Like tea leaves swirling, oh what a surprise!

My fortune's found in a teacup,
No need for wisdom, or a mix-up.
In lemon zest, I seek the norm,
While biscuits dance, the flavors swarm.

So let's tip the kettle, have no fear,
For wisdom brews with every cheer.
An ancient sage once lost his key,
Found it in the bottom of a jasmine tea!

It's just a leaf, or so they say,
Yet it helps me tackle my silly day.
With giggles floating, and cups in hand,
Together we wander, a dizzying land.

The Calm of Camellia

In the quiet of the kitchen, I smile,
Camellia's calm, let's linger awhile.
Steeping my thoughts with a dash of glee,
Who knew life's answers were brewed with tea?

The kettle sings a jovial tune,
While I ponder the stars and the moon.
With a biscuit beside, I take a sip,
And suddenly, I'm a tea-tasting trip!

Spilling leaves, the cat gives a stare,
As I find wisdom hidden somewhere.
A mug in one hand, and laughter on cue,
With each little mess, a meaning anew!

So raise your cup, let's toast with delight,
To the leaves, the laughs, from morning to night.
In this steaming world, where silliness brews,
Life's lessons sit right among the stews.

Unraveling in a Mug

Big mug in hand, life feels right,
Unraveling knots, from morn till night.
With each sip, I dance and sway,
Who needs a gym when I've got earl gray?

Stains on my shirt, but who even cares?
In the world of tea, no room for snares.
I spill my blend, but then I grin,
A canvas of colors begins to spin!

Hypothetical debates over chamomile,
Or how green tea makes my brain feel agile.
I'm the barista of my mind's little store,
With frothy ideas that I can't ignore!

So here's to the leaves that help me see,
That the riddle of life is sipped with glee.
Let's brew some fun, let's keep it light,
With each silly mug, we'll set things right!

A Symphony of Scents

A whiff of mint, a dash of spice,
The kitchen's alive, and oh, so nice!
With every sip, I hear a song,
A symphony brewed, can't go wrong!

The flavors blend, a playful tease,
I slurp like a kid, oh, it's such a breeze.
Earl grey gets jealous, while chai rolls its eyes,
As I start crooning to the sweet apple pies!

Laughter bubbles up with each tasting,
While my thoughts dance wildly, no wasting.
Finding joy in oranges and longtime chats,
As the dog rolls by—what's up with that?

So bring on the steam, let's start the cheer,
This bootleg concert warms every ear.
With blends all around, a festival's near,
In every sip, I find what I hold dear!

Brewed Reflections

With a cup in hand, I ponder deep,
How to find joy, and not just sleep.
I sip the warm brew, flavors collide,
Laughing at thoughts I can't even hide.

Is it chamomile dreams or green tea sighs?
With every sip, wisdom's disguise.
The kettle whistles, life's odd tune,
Making me wonder, do potions just bloom?

Steeping in Solitude

In my corner, a teapot sings,
Who knew solitude had such swings?
With each steep, I giggle and dream,
Caught in the joy of a whimsical theme.

Lemon and ginger dance on my tongue,
Is this what they mean when they say I'm young?
I pour, I sip, my mind's in a whirl,
What's the meaning? Oh, where's my pearl?

Sips of Serendipity

Pour another cup, let the laughter flow,
Fate's in the brew, isn't that so?
Each sip brings a chuckle, a twist in the tale,
As thoughts tumble lightly, like leaves in the gale.

Earl Grey giggles, while minty fights,
Questions and answers light up my nights.
One sip for laughter, one for the grind,
With tea in hand, I'm hilariously blind!

The Elixir of Existence

With every infusion, my soul does cheer,
Wonders of life fogged slightly by beer.
But here's a thought, with this lovely blend,
Are we tea leaves swirling, or just a trend?

Brewed like a potion, it's chaos and grace,
In this porcelain cup, I find my place.
Life's riddles unravel, one sip at a time,
Steep and repeat, Oh! Life feels sublime!

The Aroma of Dreams

A teapot whistles tunes of glee,
While I ponder what could be.
With every sip, I float on air,
Pretending life is fair and square.

Spilled a drop upon my shirt,
Suddenly, I'm a tea-stained flirt.
My mug's my guide, my silly sage,
Leading me through life's grand stage.

The steam rises, telling tales,
Of chocolate ships and lemon sails.
Teacups dancing, oh what fun!
Who knew philosophy could run?

But wait, I spilled, oh dear, oh my!
Wasn't it just tea I was to try?
Yet here I stand, a puddle near,
In this chaos, I find cheer.

Yesterday's Leaves

Left my thoughts on yesterday's brew,
Like leaves afloat, they dance anew.
A splash of honey, a slice of zest,
In whimsy's arms, I find my rest.

I brewed a storm with minty flair,
Why is my cup so light and rare?
Frothy visions swirl and spin,
Amidst this laughter, where do I begin?

The kettle simmers, soft, divine,
Turning my worries into thyme.
A dash of joy, a sprinkle of fate,
This cup's my friend, my happy state.

Yet tea bags mock with sly intent,
Am I the fool, or they, heaven-sent?
But who would swap this joyful spree?
I'll sip and smile, just let it be.

Tomorrow's Thoughts

With each new brew, I dream ahead,
A cup of hope is gently wed.
What will it hold, this coming day?
A caffeinated leap, or a tea leaf play?

The leaves of future steep and sway,
In visions brewed, I find my way.
Caffeine monsters lurk with glee,
Will they help or hinder me?

Sipping slowly, the clock does tease,
While my mug whispers 'take it easy'.
Plans like marshmallows float and dive,
In this sweet cup, I feel alive.

To sip or not to sip? Oh dear!
Immediate wisdom disappears.
But in this folly, laughter grows,
In every cup, life's banter flows.

Brews of Contemplation

In the cradle of my cozy seat,
A mug of warmth becomes my beat.
With every pour, I ponder fate,
Is it the tea, or just my plate?

Spices swirl in a dance of grace,
Twisting my thoughts, a warm embrace.
Should I add milk or go all black?
Decisions here could cause a crack!

Brewed reflections breed delight,
As I sip on hope, in the quiet night.
Tea stains my dreams in lovely hue,
Does a cup of joy not speak the true?

When life gets complex, I just steep,
Those leaves know secrets, they don't keep.
In the boiling pot, a chuckle's spun,
A sip of laughter, I've just begun.

Essence of Comfort

When the world feels like a frantic brew,
I find solace in a cup or two.
Infusions of comfort sip so right,
Bouncing through chaos, what a sight!

Murmurs of tea leaves whisper near,
"Steep your worries; have no fear!"
Yet as the kettle begins to whistle,
I drop my spoon—a funny twizzle.

Gather 'round, my friends in steam,
Life's not as tough as it might seem.
In every cup, a little cheer,
And possibly a bit of weirdness here!

So let us laugh as we sip away,
In this cozy nook, we'll happily stay.
A blend of giggles, a dash of zest,
With tea in hand, we'll face the quest.

Tea Leaves and Truths

One sip in the morning, I ponder my fate,
Is it the tea or the biscuits? I hesitate!
With each little swirl, my thoughts start to dance,
Should I brew Earl Grey or give green tea a chance?

As the kettle whistles, my wisdom's on hold,
Maybe I'll flip through the tales that are told.
What's steeped in the pot is far more than taste,
It's the giggles, the dreams, in the moments we waste.

Moments Brewed

I sit with my tea, contemplating my role,
Should I save the world or just snack on a whole?
A splash of milk here, a splash of hope there,
Stirring up laughter, forget all my care!

Each cup a reminder of life's silly game,
Like finding the sugar in a salt shaker's name.
With a grin and a sip, I let worries take flight,
In this whimsical whirl, everything feels right.

Infusions of Intent

The leaves swirl and tumble, what wisdom will brew?
A dash of perspective, a pinch of bright hue.
Should I contemplate love or just stir and sip slow?
Why not solve world peace while the kettle starts to glow?

With chamomile calm and a chuckle so light,
I brew up some joy; it's a magical sight.
The secrets of tea, like a tongue-in-cheek rhyme,
Make the chaos of life feel so perfectly fine.

A Cup of Quietude

In my cozy corner with a mug full of cheer,
I muse about life while the world disappears.
Each slurp draws a giggle, each sip a good thought,
Is it the brew or the banter I've sought?

With scones on the side, life's lessons unfold,
Like the many odd flavors of tea leaves untold.
A dash of absurdity, an ounce of delight,
In this funny little ritual, everything's bright.

Embracing Warmth

In a mug of chaos, I seek a clue,
A swirl of thoughts and a dash of brew.
Sipping caffeine dreams while I rehash,
Chasing down smiles like they're limited cash.

The kettle sings songs of my woes and cheer,
As steam paints portraits that disappear.
Each sip's a giggle, each gulp's a grin,
Pouring in laughter, I'm ready to win!

Ephemeral Sips

A teapot's a fountain of fleeting delight,
Each sip a mystery, brewed just right.
I ponder my choices, sip after sip,
Is it life's great riddle or just a tea trip?

Lemon or honey? My taste buds debate,
With marshmallow dreams that I can't quite relate.
I'm building a castle of flavors divine,
Sipping my way through this intricate line.

A Tapestry of Tastes

In a world of flavors, I tumble and roll,
With every steeped leaf, I find a new goal.
Earl Grey whispers sweet nothings to me,
While chamomile nudges, 'Just let it be!'

Jasmine is giggling, oolong joins in,
In this quirky ballet, I'm the jester with sin.
Flavors collide in an awkward dance,
As I guzzle my potion and join in the trance.

Harmony Within the Leaves

Tea leaves conspire, a clandestine crew,
Plotting to brew up some fun for a few.
A smirk from the oolong, a wink from the chai,
Together they giggle at life passing by.

With a splash and a bubble, the laughter flows free,
As I sip all my worries while clutching my tea.
In each little cup, the world feels so bright,
It's a potion of joy, back to life I take flight!

The Brew of Existence

In a cup, the world I find,
Flavors dance, both bold and blind.
Sipping dreams with a dash of glee,
Questioning all, just me and my tea.

Leaves unfurl like tales untold,
Hot water whispers, secrets bold.
If life's a brew, I've got the knack,
Stirring laughter, with no lack!

Each sip a smile, a twist of fate,
Sweet or bitter, I contemplate.
In this mug, no room for strife,
Just frothy joy, the zest of life.

So raise your cup, let worries sway,
With every gulp, thoughts drift away.
In this potion, I find my cheer,
Life's absurdity, crystal clear!

Seeking Solace in Steam

In morning light, I brew my calm,
Infused with chaos, a soothing balm.
Steam rises high, like dreams in flight,
Whisking worries with sheer delight.

Each sip, a giggle, a wink from fate,
Chasing shadows that laugh and prate.
I ponder deep, with herbs and spice,
Finding wisdom in mischief's slice.

Tea leaves joke, with flavors bold,
In every drop, a tale unfolds.
Why worry 'bout what's on the way?
Just sip it slow, let laughter play!

The world's a stage, and I a guest,
With every steep, I do my best.
So here's to brews that twist and turn,
In every sip, there's more to learn!

Reflections in a Brew

Looking deep into my cup,
I see the universe, all stirred up.
With each reflection, laughter beams,
Tea-soaked thoughts spill out like dreams.

Cups are half-full, or so they say,
But this one's brimming, come what may.
The spoon's a wand, I cast my wish,
For frothy bubbles and marshmallow bliss!

Every slurp, a gleeful sigh,
While tea leaves giggle and numbers fly.
Reality quirks with a zingy laugh,
As I sip wisdom, steeped like a craft.

Brews get stronger, but so do I,
With every gulp, I learn to fly.
So let's toast to cups, all bold and bright,
Finding our joy in the warm daylight!

The Dance of Flavor and Thought

Gather round for a tasty affair,
Where flavors dance in the fragrant air.
Cinnamon twirls with a minty spin,
As I ponder where to begin.

The kettle sings its bubbling tune,
Like a shower of stars under the moon.
Each sip is laughter, a twisty quest,
With nutty notes that make me jest.

Spices tango, a cuppa delight,
As I ponder my next silly plight.
What's the purpose? Who really knows?
Perhaps it's just this tasty prose!

So brew it warm, let bubbles roar,
In every sip, I find much more.
A dance of flavors, thoughts on parade,
With each cup shared, our worries fade!

A Lullaby of Loose Leaf

In a kettle, the bubbles play,
As I ponder my life today.
Is it green or black that feels right?
Or a spicy chai under the moonlight?

With a pinch of sugar, added for fun,
I sip my thoughts, oh, what have I done?
Brewing dreams like a master chef,
Pouring laughter, I forget my stress.

The leaves dance in their herbal swirl,
While I try to catch that elusive pearl.
Each sip reveals a hidden clue,
Is it the tea, or is it just you?

So here's to cups that tickle the mind,
With every pour, new truths I find.
A sip of joy, stir of delight,
Loose leaf lullabies into the night.

Dancing with Delicacy

In the cup, a waltz begins,
Tea leaves swirl, joy within.
With a dash of spice, a dash of cheer,
I find my rhythm, my path is clear.

A croissant on the side, soft like a dream,
Balancing breakfast, or so it may seem.
With each delicate sip, I feel my feet,
Waltzing through life, oh what a treat!

Sipping in sunshine, laughing out loud,
Grateful for moments, so proud, so proud.
Tea makes my worries feel light as air,
As I dance through my day without a care.

With petals and leaves, I spin and swish,
Life is a dance, oh, what a wish!
So toast with your teacup, join in the play,
In this delicate dance, we'll find our way.

Tea-Time Epiphanies

With a teabag, I sit and reflect,
What's the secret that I should detect?
Steeping my thoughts in waters divine,
Each sip a revelation, oh so fine.

The clock ticks down, I've lost track of time,
In a brew of confusion, I stumble and rhyme.
Why does Earl Grey seem so profound?
Is there wisdom to be found in this round?

Frothy milk and a sprinkle of spice,
Could it really be the tea's advice?
As I ponder the meaning of life and such,
It's clear to me: I'm overthinking too much!

So let's raise our cups, in toasts we cheer,
To steaming dreams, both far and near.
With each tea-time, adventures unfold,
And the secrets of life become stories told.

In Search of the Ideal Blend

In the pantry, a riot of hues,
Can I find the blend for my worn-out blues?
A pinch of this, a sprinkle of that,
Mixing my masterpiece—what do you think, cat?

Tasting lemon, ginger and zest,
Crossing my fingers, I'm hoping for the best.
Figuring out flavors, in and out of the pot,
And laughing at life, oh, that hits the spot!

In my quest for perfection, what's right or wrong?
Is it a milky dream or a herbal song?
Each sip a quest, a giggle, a snort,
Like a comedy show, never a bore!

So here's to the cups, both big and small,
In this voyage of tea, we'll conquer it all.
With every blend, a story anew,
Just remember, dear friend, I'm talking to you!

Brews of Belonging

In a mug, my troubles hide,
The leaves swirl, a joyous ride.
A sip of hope, a dash of cheer,
In this tea, I hold my dear.

Laughter bubbles, herbs collide,
Each cup is like a cozy slide.
Raise your spoon, give a cheer,
For every friend who's gathered near.

A dash of spice, a pinch of fun,
We sip and giggle, never done.
A teapot's tale, stories unfold,
In every brew, a memory told.

So let's steep our dreams tonight,
With silly chats, each brew's just right.
In this teacup, life's a game,
Pour joy, not worries—just the same!

In Search of the Perfect Pour

I wandered far for leaves just right,
In each sip, there's pure delight.
Was it green? Or chai I seek?
Oh dear tea, you're such a sneak!

With mugs stacked high, I try and taste,
These blends of magic, never waste.
The secret brew? A funny friend,
Who spills the tea as the laughter blends.

A dance of flavors, oh the thrill,
I seek that pot, I chase and spill.
Earl Grey, Oolong, they're close, it's true,
But nothing beats a laugh with you!

So here I sit with cup in hand,
And sip my way through this funny land.
Perhaps the pour is found in jest,
In every laugh, I feel the best!

Pouring Over Life's Pages

A book, a brew, a cozy chair,
Sip by sip, without a care.
Plot twists and turns, my tea can't wait,
It joins the tale—oh, isn't fate great?

With every chapter, let's not be shy,
A little sip and we'll both fly.
The tea leaves whisper stories old,
In every sip, new dreams unfold.

Oh wait, what's this? A splash of fun?
My tea confesses it wants to run!
I spill the tales, they froth and foam,
In this caffeinated literary home.

So let's brew joy and read away,
As characters dance and spices play.
With every page, we'll sip and cheer,
Life's just a story, let's make it clear!

Echoes of Herbal Harmony

In a teacup, echoes sing,
Of chamomile dreams and joy they bring.
With minty laughter, we find our way,
Sipping harmony throughout the day.

A dash of honey? Oh what a tease!
I pour the sweet and aim to please.
In every sip, a giggle hides,
Together we flow on herbal tides.

Let's brew a ruckus, let's spill the tea,
In this wacky blend, just you and me.
As laughter steeps and friendships bloom,
In our cups, there's always room.

So here's to brews that keep us light,
With every gulp, we take flight.
In herbal harmony, we find our place,
Sipping joy at our own pace!

The Journey in a Kettle

A kettle on the stove, it grumbles with glee,
Its whistle's a symphony, calling to me.
Each bubble a secret, a tale yet untold,
Of dreams steeped in warmth and adventures bold.

The water's a dancer, swirling with cheer,
It hops and it skips, like a child with no fear.
I watch as it simmers, my thoughts start to twirl,
In this cozy moment, I find my own whirl.

Oh, the leaves that I toss, they tumble and dive,
Infusing the giggles that help me to thrive.
Every sip is a chuckle, a joy wrapped in steam,
Life's riddles unwind as I brew and I beam.

So here's to the kettle, my partner in fun,
Together we ponder till the day is all done.
A splash of good humor, a dash of delight,
In the journey we share, everything feels right.

The Heart of Infusion

In a teacup, an ocean swirls under my chin,
With leaves that perform like a circus, they spin.
Each sip is a jest, a tickle of spice,
A party in porcelain, oh, isn't that nice?

The sugar's a sidekick, adding some thrill,
Together we giggle, our cups always fill.
As cream cascades down like a white fluffy cloud,
My heart starts to bounce, feeling fresh and so loud.

So I swirl with my spoon, giving life a good whirl,
Each twist is a wink, every swirl is a twirl.
The blend sings a tune, a sweet silly song,
With every small sip, I just know I belong.

Let's toast to the flavors, the clinks and the clatters,
In this world of chaos, it's laughter that matters.
With teacups held high, let our spirits take flight,
In this heart of infusion, everything feels right.

Tranquility in a Teaspoon

A teaspoon of laughter, a sprinkle of cheer,
Unlocking the joy that feels ever so near.
I measure out moments, as if they were gold,
With a flick of my wrist, life's stories unfold.

Each scoop is a giggle, joy stirred up with flair,
Swirling in my cup, floating freely through air.
The aroma tickles, like whispers of fun,
Drawing me in, oh, how I am spun!

A splash of adventure, a dash of mirth,
Brewing happiness gently, giving it worth.
With each little sip, I dance on the floor,
Lost in the moment—who could ask for more?

So here's to the teaspoon, my trusty old friend,
Together we brew till the very last blend.
In the quiet of sipping, my worries do cease,
Finding bliss in the stirrings, a tiny sweet peace.

Sip by Sip

Sip by sip, the world starts to play,
With tea in my cup, I'll dance through the day.
My worries are drowned in a sea of warm brew,
With each playful sip, I'm meeting the new.

Laughter's the flavor, each giggle a treat,
In this delightful concoction, life feels so sweet.
The swirling concoction keeps spinning my tale,
In the chaos of life, I simply set sail.

As steam rises up like a spirit on high,
I watch my thoughts dance, like clouds in the sky.
With comfort in cup and smiles all around,
Every sip is a bounce, I can't help but bound.

So raise up your teacups, let's cheer and unite,
For each silly moment, let's savor the light.
With laughter as fuel, life's a grand clip,
In the art of good brewing—drink deep and let rip!

www.ingramcontent.com/pod-product-compliance
Lightning Source LLC
Chambersburg PA
CBHW051701160426
43209CB00004B/976